Moms Moms Moms

OTHER BOOKS BY S. GROSS

How Gross

I Am Blind and My Dog is Dead

An Elephant is Soft and Mushy

More Gross

Why Are Your Papers In Order?

Dogs Dogs Dogs

Cats Cats Cats

All You Can Eat

Golf Golf Golf

Movies Movies Movies

WITH JAMES CHARLTON

Books Books Books

Moms Moms Moms

A Mirthful Merriment of Cartoons

Edited by S. Gross

HARPER & ROW, PUBLISHERS, New York
Grand Rapids, Philadelphia, St. Louis, San Francisco
London, Singapore, Sydney, Tokyo, Toronto

Grateful acknowledgment is made for permission to reprint the following:

V. Gene Myers cartoon, "Hi, Mom," in *Playboy*. Reproduced by special permission of *Playboy* magazine: Copyright © 1983 by *Playboy*.

Brian Savage cartoon, "I am the ghost of Christmas past," in *Playboy*. Reproduced by special permission of *Playboy* magazine: Copyright © 1968 by *Playboy*.

Eldon Dedini cartoon, "What's obscene to me, Myrtle…," in *Playboy*. Reproduced by special permission of *Playboy* magazine: Copyright © 1972 by *Playboy*.

Cartoons copyrighted by *The New Yorker* are indicated throughout the book.

Some of the cartoons in this collection have appeared in the following periodicals and are reprinted by permission of the authors: *Crop and Soil Management, Family Circle, Good Housekeeping, Ladies' Home Journal, Lears, National Enquirer, National Lampoon, New Woman, New York Times Book Review, Nexos Magazine, Philadelphia Inquirer Magazine, Psychology Today, Saturday Evening Post, Science, Woman's World, World*.

FIRST EDITION

Designed by Kim Llewellyn

Library of Congress Cataloging-in-Publication Data

Moms, moms, moms : a mirthful merriment of cartoons / edited by S. Gross.—1st ed.
   p. cm.
ISBN 0-06-016255-4
   1. Mothers—Caricatures and cartoons.   2. Motherhood—Caricatures and cartoons.   3. American wit and humor. Pictorial. S. Gross, S. (Sam)
NC1426.M6   1990
741.5′973—dc20   89-45664

90 91 92 93 94 HOR 10 9 8 7 6 5 4 3 2 1

For Michelle,
who made a "Mom" out of Isabelle

"Here's to moms everywhere—from Mother Macree to Mother Hubbard; Mother Nature to Mother Theresa, Mother Courage, Mother Earth, Mother Russia and even Ma Barker. God bless them all!"

SILVIO REDINGER

"She's just like her mother!"

GEORGE BOOTH

"Are you absolutely sure, Dr. Pleshke, that my mother's advice hasn't affected the treatments?"

ELI BAUER

"It's a collect call from my dear old mother!"

V. GENE MYERS

OLDDEN

RICHARD OLDDEN

"I don't care how important it is. You have to come home. Supper is ready."

BILL WOODMAN

"That's pretty serious...driving under the influence of three screaming children."

"Hi, Mom."

V. GENE MYERS

DAVID PASCAL

"Your mom's a very special person."

"I would like to trade him in for something quieter and better behaved."

"That's sweet, Sonny, but I'm not a saint. The salt of the earth, maybe."

EDWARD FRASCINO

"The Maternity Hospital—
and relax, I'm the doctor."

HELLO, PREGNANCY...

GOOD-BYE, PRIVACY!

ANNE GIBBONS

WILLIAM HOEST

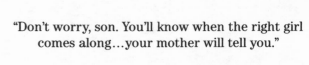

"Don't worry, son. You'll know when the right girl
comes along...your mother will tell you."

"Oh, she talks a lot…
but only about her children."

MORT GERBERG

KOREN

ED KOREN

"Do you want to talk about it?"

"When I was a frog, she was my surrogate mother."

WARREN MILLER
© 1986 The New Yorker Magazine

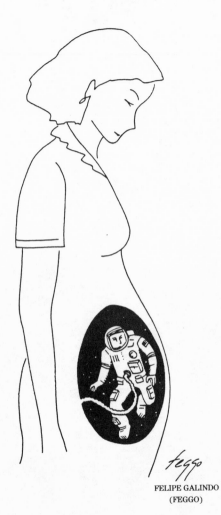

"It's true, darling, I am a kook, but first I'm a mother."

"Then at ten o'clock, you're meeting with that mothers' group that wants legislation requiring warm, dry boots to be worn when it rains."

"Out of my way, Sonny!"

"Darling!"

CHARLES ADDAMS

"It's a packed house, knock 'em dead!"

BERNARD SCHOENBAUM

"Is that Mother, dear?"

BRIAN SAVAGE

"Perhaps the realization that our youngest is 21 years old today will snap you out of your postpartum depression."

BORIS DRUCKER

"I don't care what they teach you in school, don't run
with a stick in your mouth."

FRANK MODELL
© 1988 The New Yorker Magazine

"Now do you believe me, darling? There's the proof that it does turn black and eventually falls off."

JONIK

JOHN JONIK

© 1989 The New Yorker Magazine, Inc.

Drucker

BORIS DRUCKER

"There! And now to invade the corporate board rooms, write a best seller,
hit the lecture circuit, or whatever!"

"You just have to learn to say no."

"It's good to see women going into other businesses besides pies."

AL ROSS

"You can yell your heads off. I now have aggravation insurance."

MOTHER

S. GROSS

S. GROSS

HENRY MARTIN

BRIAN SAVAGE

"I am the ghost of Christmas past."

SILVIO REDINGER

"What's obscene to me, Myrtle,
is my son wanting to stick me
away in some retirement home."

ELDON DEDINI

"Just jump in, dear. That's how your grandmother taught me to swim."

FRANK COTHAM

"Cloris, call Bob Saperstein and tell him I need the deposition by Friday, buzz Judy and have her bring me the prospectus on Miller Technologies, get Martin Ashford on the phone for me, and call Woodlawn and have them throw some flowers on my mother's grave."

"I need something smashing
for my son's wedding.
All eyes will be on me."

EDWARD FRASCINO

"I'll tell you what your mother looks like
if you'll tell me what my mother looks like."

COCHRAN!

BRUCE COCHRAN

"Those cops aren't going anywhere young man, so sit down and eat."

DAN COLLINS

"Mother, please...!"

MEL YAUK

"For the moment I've been able to convince Ralph that they're his.
I told him that when wolves are very young, they look like monkeys."

CHARLES ADDAMS
© 1972 The New Yorker Magazine, Inc.

"Why can't you be more like Oedipus?"

ARTURO POTTIER

"Darling, don't put that in your mouth, you don't know where it's been!
Put this in your mouth instead."

HURDLES.

HIGH JUMP.

JAVELIN.

100 YD. DASH TO THE SCHOOL BUS.

PUT THE IRON.

MOM'S TRACK MEET.

WOODMAN
BILL WOODMAN

"He was always a good boy, always obedient, never got into trouble. I just can't believe he would involve Hextel, Crockett, Blenham in a criminal conspiracy."

ELDON DEDINI

JERRY MARCUS

"Why do *I* always have to be the bad guy?"

"You wanted designer labels? You've got designer labels!"

JARED LEE

V. GENE MYERS

"Yes."

"Christopher, when are you going to grow up?"

MEL YAUK

"Would you mind dropping me off a block from school, Mom?"

STUART LEEDS

"You can tell *me*, Helen. What's the secret of staying so slim?"

"You're never going to make it to Florida loaded up like that."

S. GROSS

"Happy mothers are all alike.
Unhappy mothers are unhappy
in their own way. They should tango."

ELDON DEDINI

"I come to bury Caesar, not to praise him. And now to praise him,
we call forth Caesar's mother."

JERRY MARCUS

"Well, if you must know, you were pulled out of a magician's hat!"

"Wake up, Mom! We just looked at your calendar and you have nothing scheduled."

LIZA DONNELLY
DONNELLY

"Mom's happy because she got to choose the campground for tonight."

CHARLES RODRIGUES

SILVIO REDINGER

"I think we'll both have the Mother's Day special."

TIM HAGGERTY

"Oh, Mother, you think everyone's too thin."

MICHAEL MASLIN

EDWARD FRASCINO

"We've had it! It's Mother Nature!"

"Nice to see you again, Mrs. Hanover! Kids go back to college?"

"I guess that wasn't my first 'hot flash' after all, Millie."

"Mother!!"

CHARLES SAUERS

DON'T EMBARRASS YOUR CHILD BY APPEARING "OUT OF UNIFORM"! NEXT TIME, DO YOUR SHOPPING AT THE...

REAL MOM SHOPPE!

Gee, Mom! You look great!

actual hairstyle

sweater covered with lots of "cheerful" doodads

slightly flared, out-of-date, E-Z care artificial-fiber slacks

knee-high clear hose

adult pumps

THE STORE TO VISIT WHEN YOU KNOW IT'S TIME EVEN YOU STARTED LOOKING LIKE A...

REAL MOM

ROZ CHAST

"But, mother, what do *you* know about love?"

MEL YAUK

STEWART SLOCUM

"He's almost 2½. I'm almost 16½."

UNSENDABLE
Mother's Day Cards

You gave me all you had to give,
I thank you from my heart.
But frankly, Mom, I'm glad we live
A thousand miles apart.

  With mixed emotions from your
      unappreciative daughter.

You made my teen-age years so blue;
Lots of tears were spilt
Yet everytime I think of you
My head fills up with guilt.

  Sent out of a sense of duty
  by your ungrateful son.

↓ ↓ ↓ ↓

I've been in analysis for seventeen years,
Trying to deal with my deep-seated fears.
I've never blamed you, and I never will,
Nevertheless, I'm enclosing the bill.

From your confused child on
this special day.

ROZ CHAST

LEE LORENZ

"Now look what you've done!"

CHARLES SAUERS

"If I ever return to the womb, it won't be yours!"

ORLANDO BUSINO

"This is the thanks I get cooking for a large family who never show up for meals."

"My daughter, Sarah, ate all her lamb chops for dinner.
That and other nice news next at eleven."

MORT GERBERG

CHARLES RODRIGUES

"Jimmy, didn't Mama always tell you to have clean underwear on? Well, I just *hope* Justice Scalia turns down your appeal and you have to go tonight, it'll serve you right!"

"Mother! Harold's just going to put some money in the meter."

ORLANDO BUSINO

"What can we get her for Mother's Day? She already *has* an AK-47."

DONALD REILLY

"That's my mother. She's out back on the trampoline."

BORIS DRUCKER

© 1974 The New Yorker Magazine, Inc.

"Ivan is my enfant terrible!"

PETER PORGES

"Did you ever notice how you always stand up to talk to your mother?"

EDWARD FRASCINO

"Mother sends Season's Greetings with her love to you, Lydia. She says how she does so wish to spend the holidays with us but she knows that would mean we would have to drive five hundred and fifty miles to her house, as it is impossible for her to accept our invitation to come to our house, since our house, being so untidy, no offense intended, in parentheses, makes her uncomfortable to the point of actually causing her to become physically ill, but that she is willing to be a martyr all alone in order to keep everybody happy, while at the same time she is hoping with all the strength her aged bones can muster that we shall decide to drive to her house, knowing every mile of the five hundred and fifty miles that we are helping to make an old lady's heart very happy happy happy."

"Here's a thought. Instead of having your mother and my mother over for Thanksgiving dinner, why don't we stick 'em both in a cab and send 'em to Cooky's Steak Pub?"

OLDDEN

RICHARD OLDDEN

BRIAN SAVAGE

"Is this a smart move, Kathryn? Careerwise?"

SOLDIER
STATESMAN
AUTHOR
PATRIOT
BUT STILL
A
DISAPPOINTMENT
TO HIS MOTHER

MISCHA RICHTER

DONALD REILLY

"Remember what you promised Mommy—no screaming
if you stylist happens to be off."

JERRY MARCUS

"I think Fred was so considerate, he felt (drink your coffee, Helen) that it was about time (elbows off the table, Walter) that I got away from the children for awhile."

"You can't convince me she's not an unfit mother."

MARTY MURPHY

"This is real life, sweetie, you can't change mothers."

NICK DOWNES

"Let me get this straight. One bouquet goes to the mother who donated the egg. A second goes to the mother who housed the egg for insemination. A third goes to the mother who hosted the embryo and gave birth to the child. A fourth goes to the mother who raised it and a fifth goes to the mother with legal custody."

MIKE TWOHY

"You gotta be kidding!"

"Hello, Mother? I finished
'Organic Mirror.'
What should I paint now?"

EDWARD FRASCINO

VAHAN SHIRVANIAN

BILL WOODMAN

"Remember singles night?"

HOWARD MARGULIES

ORLANDO BUSINO

"I'd rather do it myself, Mother!"

BERNARD SCHOENBAUM

"Your mother was young and restless
and knew what she wanted.
She wanted out."

ELDON DEDINI

"It's hard. I have to be mother and father to them. Except on weekends when Eric has to be a father and mother to them."

SIDNEY HARRIS

"If I hear one more peep from in here I'll send for a smoker to come and get you!"

"I'm down at the lab with daddy, honey. So far we haven't decided which way we're going to make you a baby brother."

MARTY MURPHY

"Mother, dear Mother, come home with me now. Father cries
the whole night long."

ELDON DEDINI

"It's none of your business if grandpa still lights my fire."

"Honey, we're home!"

TONY ROSA

JACK ZIEGLER

GAHAN WILSON

"Actually our family has always been something
of a matriarchy."

DON OREHEK

"How would I know where you came from…
I'm your stepmother."

"Not now, dear, Mommy is freelancing!"

PETER PORGES

CHILD AT MOTHER'S KNEE
NOT LEARNING A THING

SIDNEY HARRIS

SOME MOTHERS ARE COMPULSIVE CLEANERS.

OLIVER CHRISTIANSON (REVILO)

EDWARD FRASCINO

"I get entirely too much respect. My friends complain about their indifferent and rebellious kids while I just sit there with nothing to say."

"My son here wants a job."

BUSÍNO
ORLANDO BUSINO

"I can't decide whether to have another baby or another book."

AL ROSS

" 'Hi. This is Steve. Just called to hear your new phone message. It's really funny. Well, so long.' ... 'Hi, it's Nancy. Just called to hear your message. See you.' ... 'Hi. Sammy here. Wow, great message. See you.' ... 'Hello, dear. This is Mom, and I'm a little curious. Have you lost your mind or what? Please call me.' "

JACK ZIEGLER

HENRY MARTIN

"Hi! I'm your fairy godmother with three wishes. I wish you'd sit up straight, I wish you'd comb your hair, and I wish you'd look at me when I'm talking to you."

THE HOME FOR MOTHERS
WHOSE CHILDREN HAVE DRIVEN THEM CRAZY.

MOM-IN-THE-BOX

R. Chast
ROZ CHAST

ELDON DEDINI

"See what I mean? With the kids all grown up and so much time on their hands, they don't know what the hell to do with it."

"It's a message from your mother.
She says to sit up straight and
keep your elbows off the table."

CHARLES ADDAMS
© 1985 The New Yorker Magazine, Inc.

MOM & ME.

MY MOM WOULD WHISPER UNTO ME, "CONTAIN YOUR CURIOSITY."

"I'LL LET YOU KNOW ALL KINDS OF STUFF, BUT NOT UNTIL YOU'RE OLD ENOUGH."

AND I WOULD ASK "HOW LONG TILL THEN?" SHE'D ONLY SAY, "I'LL TELL YOU WHEN."

OH, HOW MUCH LONGER MUST I WAIT? I THINK ALREADY IT'S TOO LATE.